## BRENT LIBRARIES

Please return/renew this item
by the last date shown.
oks may also be renewed by
phone or online.
Tel: 0333 370 4700
www.brent.gov.uk/libraryservice

# Transport

Written by Sally Hewitt

W

FRANKLIN WATTS

LONDON•SYDNEY

First published as *Starting Science: Transport* in 2010
by Franklin Watts. This edition 2012

338 Euston Road, London NW1 3BH

Franklin Watts Australia
Level 17/207 Kent Street, Sydney NSW 2000

**Editor:** Katie Dicker
**Art Direction:** Rahul Dhiman (Q2AMedia)
**Designer:** Shruti Aggarwal (Q2AMedia)
**Picture researcher:** Ekta Sharma, and Debabrata Sen
(Q2AMedia)
**Craft models made by:** Tarang Saggar (Q2AMedia)
**Photography:** Tarang Saggar (Q2AMedia)

**Picture credits:**
t=top b=bottom c=centre l=left r=right

**Cover:** Shutterstock
**Title page:** Cenk Unver/Dreamstime
**Insides:** Günter Lenz/Photolibrary: 6, Steve
Vidler/Photolibrary: 7t, Masterfile: 7b, Kristi
Torsak/Istockphoto: 8t, Stuart Howarth/Istockphoto:
8b, Mike Norton/Fotolia: 9bl, Greg Larson/
Istockphoto: 9br, Jo Yong Hak/Reuters: 10,
Robert Wisdom/Dreamstime: 12t, Young
Kimpark/Dreamstime: 12b, Cenk Unver/Dreamstime:
14t, Photowitch/Dreamstime: 14b, Rostislav
Glinsky/Dreamstime: 16, Bedfordshire County
Council: 18t, Japan Travel Bureau/Photolibrary: 18b,
Lim Wui Liang/The Straits Times/Contributor/
Getty Images: 20t, Javier Larrea/Photolibrary: 20b,
Stepanov/Can Stock Photo: 21, Peter Titmuss/
Alamy: 22, Jacek Chabraszewski/Istockphoto: 23,
Jose Fuste Raga/Photolibrary: 24t, Gene Chutka/
Istockphoto: 24b, Masterfile: 26, Masterfile: 27.
Q2AMedia Image Bank: Cover, Imprint page, 13, 15,
17, 19.
Q2AMedia Art Bank: Contents page, 9, 11, 13, 15,
17, 19, 25, 27.

With thanks to our models Shruti Aggarwal and
Nazia Zaidi.

A CIP catalogue record for this book
is available from the British Library

ISBN: 978 1 4451 0940 4

Dewey Classification: 388

Printed in China

Franklin Watts is a division of Hachette Children's
Books, an Hachette UK company.
**www.hachette.co.uk**

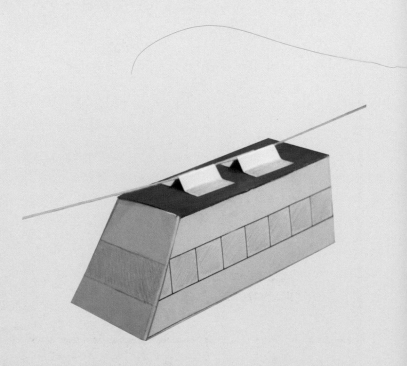

# Contents

Words that appear in **bold** can be found in the glossary on pages 28–29.

# What is transport?

Transport is the carrying of people and **goods** from place to place in vehicles. Trains, trucks, vans, cars and bicycles all carry people and goods on land. Boats travel over water and aircraft fly across the skies.

## Wheels and engines

Vehicles on wheels pulled by horses or mules have been used for thousands of years to transport people and heavy goods. Tracks and roads were built for the wheels to run along. Today, many vehicles have powerful engines that run on fuel. They carry enormous loads and lots of people.

Truck drivers fill their trucks with fuel at petrol stations. Petrol or diesel gives engines the power to work.

# Pedal power

Bicycles were invented about 200 years ago. They are cheap to use because they don't need fuel, just strong legs to push the pedals and turn the wheels. Bicycles are good for travelling short distances.

In China, many people travel to work by bike.

## A small world

Modern transport has made it possible for people to travel all over the world faster and more cheaply than ever before. A trip from Europe to Australia used to take about three months by boat. Now it can be done in less than 24 hours by aeroplane. When people travel to far away places, they learn about the traditions and ways of life in a different country.

This family is looking at holiday brochures to plan a trip away.

# Roads and bridges

Land vehicles need roads to run along. Motorways cross countries and continents, and roads link towns and cities. Small roads wind through the countryside to villages, too.

## Tunnels

Mountains, rivers, **gorges** and the sea create natural barriers for **traffic** travelling along roads. Tunnels take traffic through mountains or under gorges, rivers and the sea to cross these barriers by the shortest route.

Driving through a tunnel in the mountains makes a journey quicker.

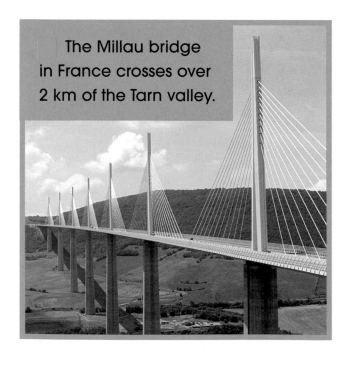

The Millau bridge in France crosses over 2 km of the Tarn valley.

## Bridges

Bridges carry vehicles across rivers, valleys, gorges and sea water. They have to carry the weight of the traffic and stay standing in high winds. Bridges made with stone and iron look solid and strong. Today, modern **materials** make strong bridges that look delicate.

# Make a bridge collage

**Design a bridge that doesn't spoil the scenery it crosses**

You will need:
- two large sheets of card • pencil • paints
- corrugated cardboard
- scissors • glue
- fine silver string

**1** On one sheet of card, draw and paint a river valley.

**2** Design your own road bridge to cross the valley. Look in books and on the Internet for ideas. You could build a bridge with stone arches or pillars, or a suspension bridge with cables, for example.

**3** Cut out the parts of your bridge from card and corrugated cardboard. Paint the parts to look like stone, concrete or metal and arrange them across your valley scene. You could cut the silver string to make some 'cables' to stick on.

How can you make the colours and shape of your bridge blend in with the surroundings?

# Long-distance trucks

Trucks carry goods over long distances. They carry materials to factories, and take items made in factories to shops to be sold. Refrigerated trucks keep food cool and fresh.

## Driving safely

Trucks are the biggest vehicles on the road. On the motorway, they keep to the inside lanes so that smaller, faster vehicles can pass them. Big side mirrors show drivers what is going on around them. Lights flash and warnings sound when a truck reverses.

## Crossing borders

Sometimes, long-distance trucks cross continents. They pass **border controls** when they drive through different countries. Border control officers check passports and the goods the vehicles are carrying.

These trucks are being checked before they drive across a border.

10

# Choose a long-distance truck route

**Choose a route for a truck carrying wood to a factory**

You will need:
- large sheet of card or paper
- pencil • felt-tip pens • string
- scissors • poster putty

1 Copy the map shown below onto the large piece of card.

2 Use the string to find the length of each route. Fix one end of the string to the timber yard with the poster putty. Now lie the string along the road following the twists and turns. Cut the end of the string when you reach the factory. Repeat for all routes.

3 Compare the length of the pieces of string. Which is the longest route? If 1 cm of string = 10 km, how long is each route?

Make a chart like the one below and then decide which route you would take. Some of the entries are done for you.

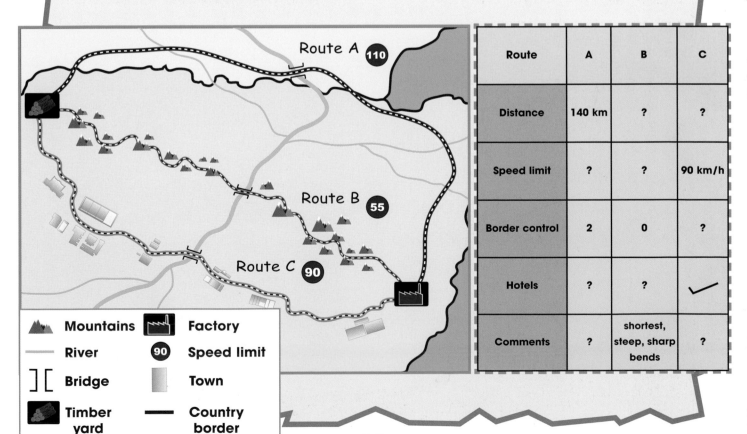

| Route | A | B | C |
|---|---|---|---|
| Distance | 140 km | ? | ? |
| Speed limit | ? | ? | 90 km/h |
| Border control | 2 | 0 | ? |
| Hotels | ? | ? | ✓ |
| Comments | ? | shortest, steep, sharp bends | ? |

**Legend:**
- Mountains
- River
- Bridge
- Timber yard
- Factory
- 90 Speed limit
- Town
- Country border

11

# Travelling on rails

Trains pulled by a **locomotive** run on railway tracks that criss-cross countries all over the world. Trains are powered by **diesel** or **electricity** and can carry many passengers.

Passenger trains have lots of carriages and carry hundreds of people.

## Trains and trams

As well as trains over land, many big cities have an underground train system. Trains pass through tunnels that run beneath busy city streets. Trams are like buses that run quickly on rails along the road. Other traffic has to stop to give the trams a clear ride.

## Maglevs and monorails

Maglevs and monorails are trains that run without burning diesel. Maglevs hover above a rail and move smoothly and silently using the force of **magnetism**. Monorails are electric trains that hang from a single rail above them.

This maglev in Australia moves people quickly into the city centre.

# Make a monorail cab

You will need:

- 2 sheets of A4 white card
- pencil • ruler • felt-tip pens
- scissors • glue or tape
- string, about 2 metres long

**1** Fold one sheet of card in half widthways and open it out. Fold each end into the centre to make four folded sections.

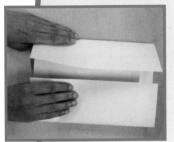

**2** Using the template below, cut one sheet of card as shown and fold along the dotted lines. Draw windows on the sides and colour the roof red. Stick the tab to the opposite side of the card to make the monorail cab.

**3** On the other sheet of card, draw round both open ends of the cab. Cut out the shapes, leaving tabs at the top and bottom. Draw on some windows. Stick the shapes to the back and front of the cab.

**4** Cut two card rectangles (5 cm x 7 cm). Fold them in half and then fold back the open ends. Stick them to the cab roof and thread the string through them. Tie the string to a cupboard handle and pull the other end taut. Lift and lower the string and watch the cab run up and down the monorail.

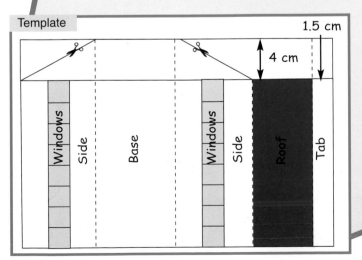

Template

1.5 cm

4 cm

Windows | Side | Base | Windows | Side | Roof | Tab

# Water transport

Ships and boats sail from **port** to port across the sea and along rivers and canals. **Cargo** ships carry enormous loads from one side of the world to another.

## Small boats

Narrowboats carry goods and people up and down man-made waterways called canals. Yachts and rowing boats are used for sport and fun. Small fishing boats bring local fish from the sea back to shore.

Yachts with colourful sails compete in a race on calm sea near to the coast.

Cranes unload containers from this ship to be transported inland.

## Big boats

Modern **passenger liners** carry holiday-makers on cruises. They stop at ports for sight-seeing along the way. Giant **tankers** carry liquids, such as water or oil, across the oceans. Container ships carry big boxes packed with goods to ports around the world.

# Transport goods around the world!

**Try this card game with a friend**

You will need:
- large sheet of card • scissors • pencil and pens

1 Cut the card into 20 playing card-sized rectangles. Divide the cards into five sets of four and draw (or label) the following onto the cards:

**Set 1:** Dubai, Sydney, oil, oil tanker
**Set 2:** Miami, the Caribbean, tourists, cruise liner
**Set 3:** Osaka, Mumbai, computers, container ship
**Set 4:** Vladivostok, Portsmouth, timber, cargo ship
**Set 5:** Vancouver, Lima, grain, bulk carrier

2 Shuffle the cards and deal five each. Keep your cards hidden from your opponent.

3 Spread the remaining ten cards face down, onto a table. The aim of the game is to get a complete set of four cards so you have the correct ship to move your cargo from port to port. Check the map to see which cards go together.

4 Take it in turns to pick up a card from the table. Turn it over to show your opponent. If you would like the card, take it and replace it with one from your pack (face down). Otherwise, turn the card back over. Try to remember where the cards are on the table. The first to get a complete set is the winner!

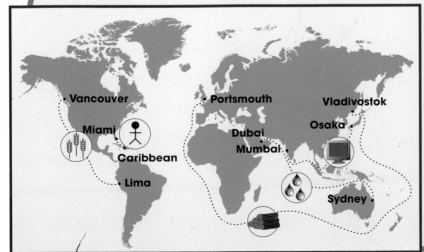

Oil tanker

# Air transport

Airliners carry passengers and their luggage and goods from airport to airport through the sky. The pilot follows a particular flight path so the skies are safe to cross.

## Airports

Airports have terminal buildings where passengers and luggage are loaded on and off aircraft. They have long runways for take-off and landing. **Air traffic control** keeps the airways safe by guiding the aircraft nearby.

## Jumbo jets

**Jumbo jets** can carry hundreds of passengers on long journeys to far away places. If all the seats are full, the price of the tickets can be kept lower. It also means fewer flights are made, so less fuel is used.

Jumbo jets travel a long way to foreign countries.

# Make a model airliner

**Ask an adult to help you with this activity**

You will need:
- large sheet of card
- pencil • scissors • paint

1 Copy the shapes onto the card, using the template as a guide. Cut them out. Ask an adult to help you to cut slits along the dotted lines in the body of the airliner.

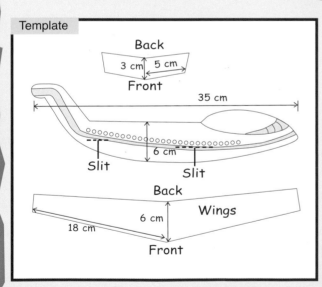

Template

Back
3 cm | 5 cm
Front

35 cm

6 cm

Slit          Slit

Back

Wings

6 cm

18 cm

Front

2 Slot the tail and the wings through the slits in the body to make your airliner.

3 Paint the parts of your airliner and let them dry. Use photographs in books or on the Internet to help you create an airline logo of your own.

4 Find out how many of your classmates have travelled by air. Record your findings on a chart. Where did they go? What kind of aircraft did they fly in?

| Destination | Aircraft |
| --- | --- |
| Italy | Boeing 737 |
| Scilly Isles | Helicopter |
| Los Angeles | Boeing 757 |

# Town-centre traffic

The roads in towns can be very busy. People make local journeys or drive through the town as they go from place to place. A road called a **by-pass** takes traffic away from the town centre.

## Park and ride

Many towns have a 'park and ride' scheme. Visitors can leave their cars in big car parks on the outskirts of a town and take a bus ride into the centre. This keeps the roads less busy and the town cleaner, with fewer **exhaust fumes** in the air.

People are taking this bus into the town centre, instead of using their cars.

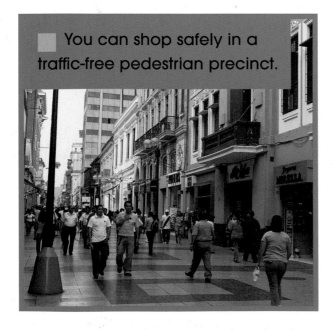
You can shop safely in a traffic-free pedestrian precinct.

## No traffic allowed!

Some towns have turned their main shopping areas into **pedestrian precincts** where no vehicles are allowed. People can shop without watching out for traffic. Other towns have bicycle lanes or bus lanes, which only bicycles or buses are allowed to use.

# Plan a traffic scheme

## Help to keep traffic out of the town centre

You will need:
- pencil • paper
- pens or crayons

1 Copy the map shown below, or make up one of your own. You could include a small town with houses, shops, surrounding roads, a river and countryside.

2 Draw in a 'park and ride' route. Where will it go? Will you need to build a new road or bridge?

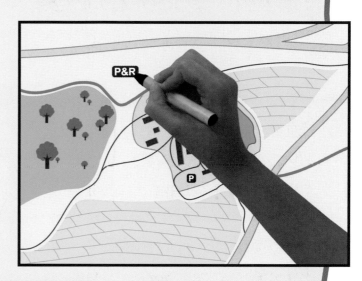

3 Choose a route between the 'park and ride' and the town. Colour it green.

4 Add a traffic-free pedestrian precinct close to some shops. Colour it in yellow.

5 Draw in a new by-pass to make the roads in the centre less busy.

Explain the route you've chosen for your 'park and ride' scheme. How will your plans affect the natural environment?

| | | | |
|---|---|---|---|
| Farmland | | ☩ | Church |
| Motorway | | | Nature Reserve |
| **P** Parking | | | Woodland |
| Houses | | | Lake |
| Shops | | | River |
| **P&R** Park and ride | | | Road |

19

# Private or public?

Many of the journeys we take are short, local journeys. We can travel by private transport, using our own cars or bicycles, or we can use public transport, such as trains, buses and trams.

## Private transport

Private cars carry people around. Vans and trucks carry work equipment and make local deliveries. Sometimes, motorbikes are used to deliver packages or take-away meals. Cyclists take their bikes out for fresh air and exercise.

This van driver is delivering a box of vegetables to a customer's house.

## Public transport

When people travel by public transport, such as buses, trams and trains, they reduce the number of vehicles used. People buy tickets for their journey. They are picked up and dropped off along a route.

Trams are a good way of taking a short journey into town.

# Do a local traffic survey

**Ask an adult to help you with this activity**

You will need:
• notebook • pencil

**1** With an adult, count the traffic at a spot near you at different times of day.

**2** Make two charts like the ones here to record your findings.

Which vehicle do you see the most?

Which vehicle do you see the least?

**3** You may be able to guess what kind of journey a vehicle is making. Can you see children with school bags in a car, or a delivery van, for example?

| Type of journey | Morning | Afternoon |
|---|---|---|
| Going to/ from work | ⊔⊔⊔⊔⊔ | \|\| |
| Going to/ from school | ⊔⊔⊔⊔⊔ \|\| | ⊔⊔⊔⊔⊔ \|\|\| |
| Shopping | \|\|\|\| | ⊔⊔⊔⊔⊔ \| |
| Delivery | ⊔⊔⊔⊔⊔ \|\|\|\| | \|\|\|\| |
| Pleasure | \|\| | \|\|\| |

What is the most common type of journey?

What is the least common type of journey?

| Traffic | Morning | Afternoon |
|---|---|---|
| Bicycle | \|\|\|\| | ⊔⊔⊔⊔⊔ \|\| |
| Motorbike | \|\|\| | \|\| |
| Car | ⊔⊔⊔⊔⊔ \|\|\|\| | ⊔⊔⊔⊔⊔ \| |
| Van | \|\|\|\| | \|\| |
| Truck | \|\|\|\| | \| |
| Bus | \|\|\| | ⊔⊔⊔⊔⊔ |

# Long journeys

People take long journeys when they go on holiday, or visit friends or family who live far away. Long journeys are also taken for work trips and delivering goods.

## Planning a journey

Long journeys need careful planning. If you are going by car, you need to plan the route using a map or the Internet. If the journey is going to take more than a day, you need to find somewhere to stay. Tickets must be booked for a trip by plane, boat or train.

## Choosing a route

When you plan a trip, there may be several different ways of getting there and back. People choose how they travel for lots of different reasons. They may want a fast journey, cheap tickets, a planet-friendly trip or one that lets you enjoy the beautiful scenery.

On a train journey, you can sit and look at the view.

# Plan a long journey

1 Choose where you want to go and find it on a map. Is your destination in the same or another country?

2 Decide why you are going there – to visit someone, to visit a place or to go on holiday?

3 Use the Internet to find out how far away your destination is.

4 Choose which types of transport you need to get there – car, bus, train, boat or plane? If you go by:

- **car** – plot your route on a map.

- **train** – which station will you depart from? Where will you arrive? Are there any changes on the way?

- **air** – which airport will you depart from? Where will you arrive?

- **water** – which port will you depart from? Where will you arrive? What kind of boat will you travel in?

Describe why you have chosen your method of transport and your destination. For example:

*I am going to Paris by train. I really want to go through the Channel Tunnel. We can see the scenery on the way to London. I want to see the Eiffel Tower when I get to Paris.*

Bus 69 from Hagley Road to Birmingham New Street station (20 minutes).
Depart Birmingham New Street 10.10.
Arrive London Euston 11.34.
Walk to London St Pancras (10 minutes).
Depart London St Pancras 12.29.
Arrive Paris 15.50.
Take Metro into central Paris.

# Keeping safe

There are rules of the road, air and water for drivers, pilots and passengers to follow. They help to prevent accidents and keep travellers safe as they travel from place to place.

## On the road

Drivers must obey speed limits for safety. In towns and cities, low speed limits protect pedestrians. Signs, lights and markings on the road give safety instructions. Drivers and passengers must always wear seat belts.

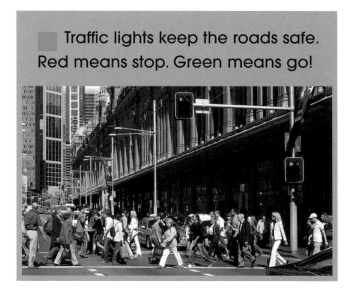

Traffic lights keep the roads safe. Red means stop. Green means go!

## Safety instructions

On some journeys, passengers are asked to listen to safety instructions or to read a leaflet. They learn how to keep safe during a journey and what to do in case of an accident. There are lifeboats and lifebelts on board a ship. Passengers can pull a cord or handle to stop a train in case of an emergency.

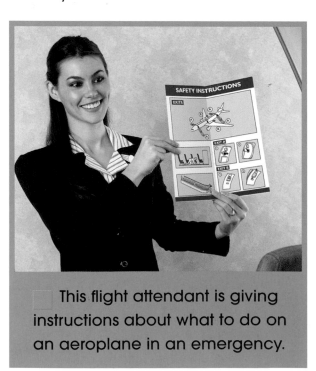

This flight attendant is giving instructions about what to do on an aeroplane in an emergency.

# Design a traffic safety leaflet

Design a safety leaflet for drivers, cyclists, and adults and children walking to and from your school.

Get to school safely!

## Children

- Always cross the road at the pedestrian crossing.
- Don't walk in the road or near the edge of the pavement.
- Look out and listen for cars, bicycles and other vehicles.

## Cyclists

- Stick to the cycle lanes.
- Wear a helmet.
- Look out and listen for pedestrians.
- Give clear hand signals.

Here are some safety instructions you could include:

## Drivers

- Don't park near our school gates.
- Drive slowly past our school.
- Don't reverse or turn near our school.

Stick to the cycle lanes.

Always cross the road at the pedestrian crossing.

# Planet-friendly travel

Transport can harm the planet. Vehicles burning fuel send exhaust fumes into the air that make it dirty. They also help to heat up the planet, which can lead to **global warming**.

## Saving energy

Walking and cycling are good ways to get fit and healthy. These forms of transport are also **eco-friendly**. We use our own **energy** so no petrol or diesel is burned. Travelling by bus or train saves fuel because one vehicle can carry lots of people at a time.

Walking is an eco-friendly way to travel to school.

# Eco-cars

New cars are being designed that are kinder to the planet. Cars can be adapted to run on **bio-fuel** instead of petrol made from oil. Electric cars run on batteries and don't send out exhaust fumes. Soon, cars with **solar panels** may be made. They use the Sun's energy.

■ An electric car is recharged, instead of filling it up with petrol.

# Design an eco-friendly vehicle

1 Design a planet-friendly vehicle for the future. Use the example on the right for ideas.

- How many people will it carry?
- What kind of fuel or power does it run on?
- What is it made of?
- Is it clean or will it send out fumes?

2 Draw and label your design (right). Can you make a model of your design from everyday materials?

**Example**

*A sports car has been made from plant fibres – the body from potato fibres, the seat from soya beans and the steering wheel from carrot fibres. Its fuel is a mixture of vegetable oil and chocolate. Fumes are cleaned before they go into the air.*

**Body made of recycled plant materials**

**Battery charged by electricity from solar panel**

**Cleaned fumes enter air**

**Space for seats in the back**

# Glossary

**air traffic control**

Air traffic control is a service that makes sure aircraft take off and land safely.

**airliner**

An airliner is a large aircraft that carries passengers.

**bio-fuel**

Bio-fuel is a type of fuel made from plants.

**border control**

Border control is where traffic is checked at a country's border.

**by-pass**

A by-pass is a road that carries traffic around a village, town or city instead of through its centre.

**cargo**

Cargo is the goods carried by trains, trucks, aircraft and ships.

**diesel**

Diesel is a type of fuel made from petroleum (oil).

**eco-friendly**

Things that are eco-friendly do less harm to the planet than things that are not eco-friendly.

**electricity**

Electricity is a type of energy we use to make things work.

**energy**

Energy is the power that makes things work. Petrol gives vehicles the energy to move.

**exhaust fumes**

Exhaust fumes are gases sent into the air by vehicles that burn fuel.

**global warming**

Global warming is the rise in the Earth's temperature. It is partly caused by burning fuels such as petrol and diesel.

**goods**

Good are items transported by trains, trucks, aircraft and ships, such as coal or food.

**gorge**

A gorge is a deep, narrow valley carved out of rocks by a river.

**jumbo jet**

A jumbo jet is a large aircraft with a wide body that can carry lots of passengers or very big loads.

**locomotive**

A locomotive is the part of a train containing the engine. It pulls the rest of the train along the tracks.

**magnetism**

Magnetism is a force that attracts objects made of metal, such as iron.

**materials**

Materials are what things are made of. Cotton, iron and wood are all types of materials.

**passenger liner**

A passenger liner is a large ship that carries passengers across the sea from port to port or on holiday cruises.

**pedestrian precinct**

A pedestrian precinct is an area in a town with shops, for people to walk around. Most vehicles are banned from entering.

**port**

A port is a place by the coast or a river bank where boats can load and unload people and goods.

**solar panel**

A solar panel collects energy from the Sun to heat water or to make electricity. In the future, cars could be powered by solar panels.

**tanker**

A tanker is a truck or a ship designed to carry liquids, such as milk or oil.

**traffic**

Traffic is the amount of cars and other vehicles on a road.

# Index